Practical Guide to
Handwriting Analysis

Practical Guide to

Handwriting Analysis

Kirsten Hall

BLACK DOG
& LEVENTHAL
PUBLISHERS
NEW YORK

TABLE OF CONTENTS

INTRODUCTION

I doubt that any of you—my readers—could convince me that you are not reading this book to learn more about yourself. Sure, you'll get around to analyzing other people's handwriting later... but first and foremost, isn't it really about me, me, me? There's absolutely nothing wrong with that. It makes more sense for you to be honest about your motives up front because as soon as your pen hits that paper, you'll find out exactly how self-involved you really are!

This book will teach you things about yourself that you may never have realized. It will also reveal aspects about you that you may not have wished to realize. You can run but you can't hide. You can close the book and put it away, or you can face the truth. That is purely your decision.

Should you opt to continue, I warn you, you will soon grapple with serious questions: Are you the person you really wish to be? Are you trapped in the past, content with the present, or obsessively anticipating the future? Are you honest with yourself and with others? Are you happy? Are you in the right career?

Annoying self-revelations aside, once you realize how much fun handwriting analysis can be, you'll want to practice your newfound skills on other people. Is your brother really happily married? Is your daughter honestly enjoying her freshman year at college, or is she keeping the truth from you—that she is terribly homesick and overwhelmed? Soon enough, you'll have answers to these questions and more.

At the end of chapters 2 through 13 in this book, you'll find portions of a handwriting sample submitted by Dotti. I encourage you to study Dotti's handwriting; try to analyze her character by applying the techniques you will be learning. Dotti's complete handwriting sample is printed at the back of the book along with my character analysis of Dotti. Why not test your skills by comparing our results?

Get out the tools of the trade—magnifying glass, Spacing Gauge and Emotion Quotient Gauge—and be prepared to wonder. Be prepared to learn. Be prepared for surprises. And have fun!

HANDWRITING ANALYSIS

CHAPTER ONE

Graphology

GRAPHOLOGY

The study of handwriting analysis is known as *graphology*. Graphology relies on the expressive nature of a person's handwriting as a means of gaining insight into his or her character, personality traits and special qualities.

Graphologists have assigned a meaning to each and every pen-stroke variation. Since the handwriting of each individual is unique, graphologists can reach their conclusions by analyzing the individual differences in the writing. The likelihood of two people having identical handwriting is one in 68 trillion.

APPLICATIONS

There are many ways in which graphology has proven itself useful: the study of child development, career placement services, psychological counseling, jury screening, criminology, compatibility assessments, the diagnosis of disease, the determination of levels of intelligence, the assessment of substance abuse, company personnel tests and many more applications.

It is important to note, however, that there are some things that handwriting analysis will not reveal. It cannot, for example, be used to determine the age or sex of the subject. In order to make an accurate analysis, a graphologist will need to know this information in advance.

Graphology must never be confused with clairvoyance. Graphologists are neither fortune-tellers nor prophets. It is absolutely not possible to predict a person's future by examining his or her writing. Handwriting analysis only reveals information about a person's present and past self.

It is also crucial to understand that, while graphologists can extract very precise character profiles from writing samples, each of us makes slight changes in our writing depending on how we feel at the moment of writing; emotions, moods and external circumstances—such as where we are, what writing instruments we are using, what we are writing about and to whom we are writing— can precipitate changes in our writing styles.

Despite these inconsistencies, a well-trained graphologist can determine a startling amount of information about a person through his or her writing. This knowledge is two-fold: about the subject's external self (how one wishes to be perceived) and about the subject's inner self (who one really is.)

Aristotle, a Greek philosopher who was born in 384 B.C. and was known as one of the greatest thinkers of all time, is believed to have said: "Spoken words are the symbols of mental experience, and written words are the symbols of spoken words. Just as men have not the same speech sounds, so all men have not the same writing."

The next piece of documented historical evidence of graphology is from the year A.D. 120, when a Roman historian of the first twelve Caesars, Suetonius Tranquillus, distrusted the Emperor Augustus based on a sample of his writing. Tranquillus was quoted as saying: "He doesn't separate his words—I do not trust him."

During the 11th century, Jo-Hau, a Chinese philosopher, stated: "Handwriting infallibly shows us whether it comes from a vulgar or noble-minded person."

The earliest publication on the subject of graphology is thought to have been *Ideographia*, a book written by an Italian scholar named Alderius Prosper in the early 17th century. A few years later, also from Italy, came Camillo Baldi's *How to Judge the Nature and the Character of a Person from His Letter*. During this same period, a group of French clergy pursued serious studies of the relationship between handwriting and personality.

Interest in graphology seems to have waned after this point, and it was more than two hundred years later when a Frenchman named Jean Hippolyte Michon began to study the work done by these clergymen. Michon gave the field of graphology its name in 1871–*Graph* being Greek for "writing" and *ology* being Greek for "the study of."

Late in the 1800s a group of German scholars grew interested in determining the accuracy of handwriting assessment depending on whether the writing was spontaneous or deliberate. Dr. Ludwig Klages, a German philosopher, concluded from his research that graphologists were consistently accurate only when the writing sample provided by the subject had been written in a spontaneous fashion.

In 1897, Dr. Klages was a pioneer in the establishment of the German Graphological Society, which delivered a monthly publication devoted to new findings in the field of graphology. A few years later, Klages was responsible for a major schism between French and German graphologists resulting from fundamental differences in their interpretation of basic rules of handwriting assessment.

In the early 20th century, graphology arrived in the United States; thirty years later, it appeared in England. Since then, it has gradually begun to receive respect as a reliable means by which to determine important insights into a subject's personality and character. While the evolution of graphology in the United States has been slow, it has nonetheless been steady.

CHAPTER TWO

Form

FORM

First impressions are powerful. We see a person's handwriting and react to its overall appearance, which graphologists call the form. Analyzing the form of a handwriting sample can yield surprisingly deep insights into a person's nature and temperament. The major form styles are: simplistic, copybook, controlled, artistic and counterfeit.

SIMPLISTIC

I like ice cream Sandwiches before I go to bed. French Fries are good too.

Ellen's writing is simple, clear and legible. Ellen is unpretentious and feels no need to add adornments to her writing. Simplistic form can be a sign of modesty, intelligence and objectivity. People who are satisfied with the essentials write with a simplistic form. Most likely, Ellen is thrifty, lives modestly and is unassuming.

I am really looking forwar
you in April. Please let me
I can bring anything for
kids. Hope all is well.

Copybook form is the method of writing taught in elementary school.
Though technically correct in style, when used by adults, it implies a
lack of creativity. Shana appears not to have added personal touches
and adjustments to the handwriting she learned in school. Perhaps she
is insincere and hides behind a formula. Alternatively, she may simply
not wish to express her individuality.

SEVERAL PEOPLE IN THE FAMILY
WERE INSANE. "CRACKERS" THEY'D
CALL THEM. IT WAS NO WONDER,
THEREFORE, WHEN TWO COUSINS MARRIED

Graham's writing is not just neat, it is meticulous and tightly disciplined. Clearly, he writes slowly and with much effort. Graham's scrupulous style tells us that he carefully considers his thoughts and actions. He thinks before he speaks and looks before he leaps. Graham's not likely to behave spontaneously. Instead, he is the type to speak and act in a deliberate fashion. He's not the friend you'd think to grab at the last minute for an unplanned adventure!

Can't wait to hear all about Your new job!

The overall appearance of Ursula's handwriting is attractive. Although quite decorative, it is still entirely legible. The occasional inconsistencies in her handwriting reveal that she writes with a natural and quick pace. Hence, we can assume that Ursula has a high level of intelligence and that she is a creative type.

Ever since my youth,
I aspired to be a cereal killer
I started with Cheerios and
then went on to Special K.

The counterfeit form serves to disguise the writer's true nature. Jean's handwriting is riddled with frills and loops—flourishes that actually hide her insecurities. Jean does not easily reveal her inner self, and it's safe to assume that the content of her writing is either weak or dishonest.

What is your first impression of Dotti's handwriting sample, shown below? Try to identify the form of her script and consider what it might reveal about her nature. My complete analysis of Dotti's handwriting samples begins on page 118.

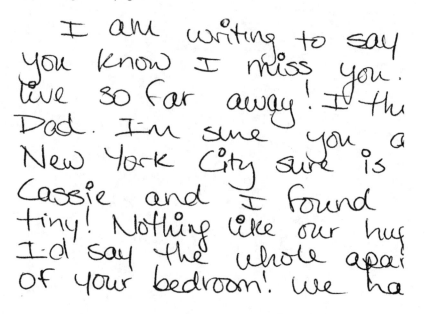

I am writing to say
you know I miss you.
live so far away! I th
Dad. I'm sure you a
New York City sure is
Cassie and I found
tiny! Nothing like our hug
I'd say the whole apai
of your bedroom! we ha

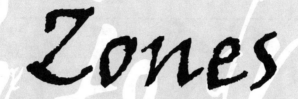

CHAPTER THREE

ZONES

THE UPPER ZONE

THE MIDDLE ZONE

THE LOWER ZONE

Looking a little beyond the overall appearance of a handwriting sample, you'll notice that the letters occupy three zones: upper, middle and lower. An emphasis on any one zone can say volumes about someone. People whose script emphasizes the upper zone, for example, are very different from those whose handwriting is heavy in the lower zone.

Many graphologists consider the three zones of writing in terms of time. The lower zone is associated with the past, the middle zone with the present and the upper zone with the writer's feelings about the future.

Graphologists also examine the three zones of handwriting relative to the human body. The upper zone equates with the upper body, the middle zone with the middle body and the lower zone with the lower body.

The only way I can get all of my work done is if I don't sleep for a

What percentage of each letter occupies the upper zone? The answer can reveal how intelligent, creative and spiritual one is. Because the letters in Zoe's upper zone are high, or extended, we know that she is intelligent, spiritual, imaginative and creative. Sometimes, an extended upper zone indicates that the writer is pretentious and domineering. Because Zoe's writing is normal-sized, however, we know that is not the case for her. Had her handwriting been abnormally large, then we could have assumed that her ego was, indeed, overly inflated.

me know if you think we've captured the essence of the product. Please don't feel like you have to edit— Just let me know if all

Angelica's letters occupy more of the middle zone than either of the other two zones. Because the middle zone pertains to a person's self-confidence, we can assume that she is secure with herself. An extended middle zone is also a sign of a person's concern with the present. Most likely, Angelica is more concerned with today than the past, and often loses sight of where she will be tomorrow. When the middle zone is small in proportion to the other two zones, the writer may be humble, cautious and even-tempered.

I'm so glad to hear
baby are in good health.
Wish your family's new year
peace in 1999. Congratulations

The lower zone signifies a person's physical self and needs. Most often the lower zone tells a graphologist about a person's sexual drive and/or concern with materialistic things. Rich's handwriting shows an emphasis on the lower zone. He's likely to be very focused on his bodily needs. Physical fulfillment and pleasure are of utmost importance to Rich. Food, sex and material goods drive his life.

Does Dotti's handwriting seem top heavy? Maybe it seems to you that
her script is very balanced, with the letters occupying equal amounts of
space in each zone. Looking at her handwriting with zones in mind, you
may begin to wonder what kind of person she really is.

I'd say the whole apart
of your bedroom! we have
bathroom, Kitchen, bedroom,
dining room. And our apar
any of our friends! Cassie
most of the decorating. Yc
that kind of stuff. So far
of her artwork, and some
white photographs. We were

CHAPTER FOUR

Baseline

BASELINE

There are two ways that graphologists (or you!) can assess a writer's baseline. If the paper on which your subject has written is lined, you can look at the writing in terms of how it appears in relation to the line. Does the writing stay consistently on the line? Does it slant upward or downward from the line?

If the paper on which your subject has written is not lined, use the Spacing Gauge provided and slide it down from the top of the page so that it rests underneath the line of writing you wish to analyze. How does the writing appear in relation to the line you have given it?

A graphologist uses the baseline of a handwriting sample to determine whether the writer is optimistic or pessimistic. The baseline affords the graphologist information regarding the writer's outlook on life.

It is important to be aware that a person's baseline is subject to change and is greatly affected by temporary moods or experiences. When using the baseline to form an accurate assessment of a person's general disposition, it is best to consider several different handwriting samples written at different times.

I am looking forward to meeting the new member of the family soon.

An upward slant to the right represents optimism. Bob's upward slant says that he is energetic and feels good about himself. Such a slant is a sign of elation, delight, self-assurance and—quite frequently—success.

You've had! And it gets
better and better.
We'll be able to come
see you early next year.

The opposite of the upward slant to the right, a downward slant is
indicative of pessimism. Gail's downward slant implies that she feels
dissuaded, daunted, exhausted or depressed. Her general outlook is one
of disappointment and frustration. Gail's attitude is pretty negative,
and she expects defeat. It's no wonder that she just lost her third job
this year.

Every time he called I said that
I really couldn't get it done in
time but he kept insisting that

A convex arc in a handwriting sample tells a graphologist that the
subject felt enthusiastic when the writing began and then grew
disillusioned as the arc fell. Many handwriting analysts equate the
use of this type of arc with people who are quitters. Quick to
abandon assignments or situations that become troublesome,
James is known to his co-workers as unreliable.

WE STAYED WITH SOME FRIENDS
IN MALIBU FOR A WHILE. THE ROADS
KEPT FALLING APART AND SOMETIMES
IT TOOK HOURS FOR US TO GET DOWN
THE CANYON.

Helena's concave, or dish, arc shows that she began writing with a negative feeling and then overcame her pessimism. Graphologists attribute a concave arc to a person who may not be the type to initiate projects or ideas, but who is best equipped to complete them. Helena, according to her supervisors, makes a wonderful editorial assistant.

Use the Spacing Gauge to figure out which baseline Dotti favors. If you
choose the same one I did, our analysis of Dotti's general outlook on life
will be similar.

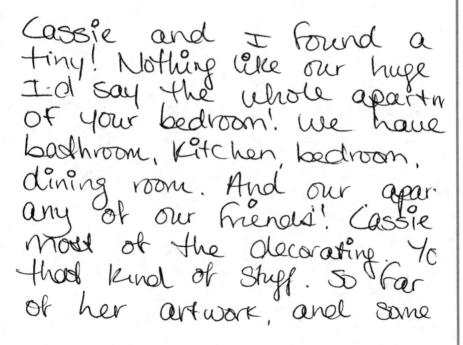

Cassie and I found a
tiny! Nothing like our huge
I'd say the whole apartm
of your bedroom! We have
bathroom, Kitchen, bedroom,
dining room. And our apar
any of our friends! Cassie
most of the decorating. Yo
that kind of stuff. So far
of her artwork, and some

CHAPTER FIVE

Pressure

Handwriting is certainly a tactile activity. When pen meets paper, some degree of force is operating. Graphologists call it the pressure and often consider it a significant indicator of a person's drive and stamina. To evaluate the amount of handwriting pressure a subject uses, have him or her write with a ballpoint pen. Then, like an expert graphologist, you can feel the back of the paper to determine if any indentations have been made.

Writing pressure is grouped into the following six categories: very light, light, normal, heavy, very heavy and inconsistent.

Be extra careful when analyzing pressure. Since writing pressure varies according to the mood of the writer, an accurate analysis cannot be made from a single sample. Ideally you should work with several samples written at different times.

What an interesting project!
Will you tell me the analysis of.
Good luck!

Kristina writes with very light pressure. This is often an indication that someone is timid and shy. Very light handwriting can also signify lethargy, powerlessness or an illness such as arthritis.   It is, however, important to examine other aspects of a person's writing before drawing any firm conclusions.

as they might, it always came ong. — so I simply changed relling and they all do fine u

Meredith's light handwriting confirms what her friends say—she is passive and gentle. She doesn't want to be the center of attention and prefers to work behind the scenes. Light handwriting can also be associated with low self-esteem, but don't make that assumption without checking your subject's personal pronouns and signatures.

sees it, really likes it. We are so pleased to have met you at the 100-acre Wood! We hope you will come by & see us during your trip to the Fla. Keys at

Kenny writes with normal pressure. A heavier downstroke than upstroke indicates that he is both mentally and physically healthy and has an impressive amount of stamina. It also tells us that when given a task, Kenny is likely to complete it. Kenny is an effective worker and is highly productive.

but coming at this time makes it so.
I've thought through many angles trying
to make it happen but the logistics of
getting there from this island to Sharm, C
is making it imposible. However, I un
certainly be with you in spirit and sad,
not to be there in person.
When I return to New York in Septm.
my first social engagement will be hostess...
Much love and hugs

Jackie's writing pressure is heavy. Based on an analysis of several samples, we can say that she is intense, forceful and confident. Since heavy pressure is associated with people who are passionate, she's probably a leader in her chosen field of interest.

I wish you had called me you were in town. I heard you were here from Michelle and was surprised that yo hadn't tried to see me.

Samuel exerts very heavy pressure when writing. After analyzing several samples of his handwriting, we can say that he often feels frustrated and aggressive. Very heavy pressure can also be a sign of excessive force or hostility. If the writer's pressure has ripped through the page at any point—beware! Jack the Ripper's handwriting pressure was very heavy. Need I say more?

ing, feeling and spirit, betray all these ge a mai

Grant's writing pressure is inconsistent—sometimes heavy, other times light and occasionally moderate. This is a sign of indecision. Indeed, Grant has never been able to commit or make up his mind—try taking a trip with him to Blockbuster Video sometime!

Grant's pressure tells us that he is overwrought and tense. Some graphologists equate uneven pressure with pacing, like walking back and forth repeatedly expressing nervous energy.

You won't be able to hold Dotti's original handwriting sample and actually
feel the pressure she used on the paper. So here's a clue: When I held the
sample, I felt an even amount of pressure throughout; the downstroke was
relatively heavy, but the overall pressure wasn't too heavy. Now what does
that tell you about Dotti?

we've made a lot of friends
our jobs. Her art is really
is having an exhibit in soh
you and Dad could come
couch in the living room. Ho
Little Chip? It's been so long
from them. Tell them to call
are my brothers, after all. S
are great! We're planning

CHAPTER SIX

Slant

SLANT

It's time to get out the Emotion Quotient Gauge and measure some angles. The slant of a person's handwriting may seem obvious to you, but it's such an important indicator of personality that you should examine it precisely. To avoid making simplistic assessments of a person's character, you'll need to analyze several samples written over a period of time.

The slant helps graphologists analyze how expressive a subject is in terms of emotion. It can also reveal the subject's attitude toward and relationship with the past, present and future. Graphologists categorize the slant of a person's handwriting according to one of the following four groups: vertical slant, inclined slant, reclined slant and inconsistent slant.

> i just wanted to send
> you a few pictures - they
> dont do justice to the
> view in Cabris but hey
> we got some good shots
> of the cacti!

Claire's vertical slant is a sign of independence, and it is evidence that she does not like to show her emotions. She trusts her own judgment and does not feel a need to share her every thought with others. Claire is an objective thinker, more interested in facts than supposition. She also lives in the present, seldom bemoaning the past or concerning herself unduly with the future.

When ever I spin forward and imaging myself curmbing, I end up in a painting by Dali heading downhill.

Fiona

People who write with a rightward slant have no compunction about expressing themselves or sharing their emotions. An inclined slant, like Fiona's, is indicative of a strong libido. Fiona is passionate and unrestrained. According to Fiona, everyone should know just how she's feeling. And she'll be the first to let you know. Hope you can spare a few hours! The inclined slant also signifies a person whose thoughts are geared toward the future.

I thought the test was very
I went to meet with the te
afterwards.

An overly inclined slant is a sign of egotism. Don't bother telling Gina if you have a problem—she's too self-absorbed to even listen. If you need to talk about anything that concerns you, your best bet is to find a friend with a less inclined slant.

yorself in the Big Bad Apple. All is
enjoying opending all of this
Getting plenty of "exercise" too
a change. I will be here until
leave for San Fran. Then on the
here and will head back to Fla at

John writes with a leftward reclined slant. Such writing is unnatural
and contradicts the motion of writing, which moves in a forward
fashion. Contrary to common supposition, a left slant is not typical of
left-handed writers. It is true, however, that a reclined slant is more
typical of women than of men. John is challenging that which is
conventional. He resists change and prefers to be oriented in the past.
In terms of self-expression, John not only conceals his emotions from
others, but is unaware of them himself.

and since then I have alwa
wondered how he is doin
If you hear from him any.
soon can you give him my re
telephone number and/or add

As you probably guessed, a writer with an inconsistent slant sometimes dwells in the past, at other times is concerned with the present and then may suddenly become obsessed with the future. Jenny's slant changes throughout a single sample. Sometimes Jenny wants everyone around her to know how she feels while at other times she will clam up and refuse to express herself. It's pretty tough to be Jenny's friend. One minute you're not interested enough; the next, you're prying and invading her space.

I went to the store to buy store books for the project but they did

When analyzing an extreme slant, consider the explanations given earlier for the reclined slant and the inclined slant, and then exaggerate the personality characteristics associated with each slant. People who write with an overly reclined slant, for example, will not be merely oriented in the past but perhaps unable to function in present-day reality.

Here's a tip for using the Emotion Quotient Gauge to measure the angle of Dotti's script: Place the plastic gauge above the sample of writing you wish to assess. Make sure (even doubly and triply sure) that the baselines of both the writing and the EQ Gauge are parallel. Now, match the slant of the writing with one of the slants labeled on the gauge. Do you think she has an inclined slant or a vertical slant or neither? You can learn quite a bit about Dotti from her slant. I wonder if you and I came to the same conclusion.

teach Kindergarten again
nothing is definate yet
class this year. we have
5 or 6. Mom, the kids
from the kids at home!
bigger and more worldly
Olivia - seems to know

CHAPTER SEVEN

Letter Size

LETTER SIZE

Graphologists care a lot about letter size; they're detail-oriented people. They also sometimes tell us things we don't want to hear. For example, after examining the letter size in several samples of my own writing, one graphologist was able to give me an accurate asessment of both how I feel in social situations and my ability to concentrate.

Several variables can affect the size of letters, two of the most common being the writer's mood at the time the sample was written and the size of the paper used. For this reason, it is important to evaluate a series of writing samples made over time in order to make an accurate assessment of the subject's personality and character.

Try to get samples written on lined 8 1/2" by 11" (20cm x 27.5cm) paper, since writing done on index cards, note cards or postcards could very well be smaller than usual and, therefore, not a fair representation of the subject's typical style.

Be not afeared, the isle is full of noises, sounds
and sweet airs that give delight and hurt not.
Sometimes a thousand twangling instruments will
hum about mine ears, and sometimes voices
that if I then had waked after long sleep
will make me sleep again; and then, in dreaming,
the clouds methought would open and show riches
ready to drop upon me that when I waked,
I cried to dream again.

Exceptionally small writing indicates an ability to focus intensely,
though it sometimes can be a sign of a reclusive person. Liza's very small
writing indicates an ability to concentrate deeply. It can also indicate a
writer who does not like to impose herself. Indeed, Liza characterizes
herself as a loner and a thinker.

know your not living at this address but I don't know your other one. Are you still living w/ Kate and Joanna? Tell them I said "hi". I just returned from a 2 in the south of New Zland where I saw the most lakes, mountains, beaches, and rainforest. Now I'm back up

Small writing, in general, is a reflection of deep concentration and is often associated with those involved in science or math. Jerry, who I later learned is a chemist, was concentrating intently when he wrote his sample. Though not exactly a recluse, he prefers time alone rather than being part of a big crowd. Jerry is the kind of guy who gets things done—and does them well. (Small writing can also reflect a writer's environmental awareness and concern about not wasting paper.)

Congratulations on your big December present! It has been great fun just going over to your apartment this

Frederick's medium writing size is considered ideal. Based on the size of his letters and his garland connections (see chapter 10), we know he has no difficulty concentrating and can assume that he has a healthy and active social life. People like Frederick, whose letter size fits into the medium category, generally are quite capable of adjusting to changes—whether personal or professional. Frederick, as it turns out, has had to move several times in the past four years. He fits in and is happy wherever he goes.

Ophelia what? Ophelia way out of the dark room? Ophelia way into a crowd? Come on. I have feel it I have feelings! Ophelia

Ophelia's large handwriting (a characteristic often associated with those who work in the arts) indicates she is extroverted and enjoys socializing. Indeed, she loves being in the spotlight and is known to her friends as the life of the party. Ophelia likes to travel and explore. One month she's climbing mountains and the next she's planning an African safari. Her large writing, decorated with fancy loops and ornamentation, tells us that she can be, at times, extreme and excessive. She's a woman with a mission, and she knows what she wants.

me know if you thin we've captured the essen of the product. Please de feel like you have to edit—

Terry's extremely large writing is consistent with his love of attention. He not only enjoys the spotlight, he lives for it! For Terry, who is a pure exhibitionist, it is essential that other people consider him important. He nearly blew his whole savings account when he threw that last open house. But what a party. (Now he'll be living on tuna fish for the next three years.)

The Spacing Gauge can help here. Most graphologists agree that medium-sized letters are characterized by a middle zone about 1/8" (3-4 millimeters) high. Use the gauge to determine the height of the middle zone. After you decide what letter size Dotti uses, try drawing some conclusions about her.

We've made a lot of friends
Our jobs. Her art is really
is having an exhibit in So
you and Dad could come
couch in the living room.
Little Chip? It's been so
from them. Tell them to
are my brothers, after all.
are great! We're planning

CHAPTER EIGHT

Spacing

SPACING

You may need the Spacing Gauge to measure spacing, which is analyzed according to the distance between letters, between words and between lines. Graphologists sometimes use spacing to help assess a subject's emotional maturity.

BETWEEN LETTERS

NORMAL

This is a sample of my handwriting

Spacing that does not strike a reader as unnatural or irregular falls into the category of normal. Relative to the size of the letters, the space between them just looks right. People like Johnny, who space their letters and words normally, are generally comfortable with others. Johnny's spacing also tells us that he thinks and writes naturally and fluidly. Transferring his ideas and thoughts into words and onto paper comes easily.

NARROW

If you have time to take the dog out for a quick
I would really appreciate it. I've got a doctor's appoint
be home until early evening. - Georgia

Georgia leaves little room between her letters and her words. She does
not have a clear understanding of boundaries and often infringes on the
personal space of others. Indeed, Georgia recently admitted that she
lost a good friend by being too overbearing. Narrow spacing sometimes
can be associated with intolerance and nervousness.

WIDE

Hope to see you on Boxing Day. Meanwhile, here's a

Rachel's wide spacing is a sign of independence. She keeps her distance both mentally and physically from those around her, even her closest friends. Rachel probably is somewhat of a loner and can sometimes be distrustful of others.

INTRRRSTED IN THE

STUNNING FLORIDA

ARCHITRCTURR.

I HAVR TO ADMIT,

THR BRRCH IS CLRRN

AND WONDRRFUL WITH

NOT MRNY PROPLR. MOSTLY

Though Gabriel wrote his sample on a piece of unlined paper, the spacing between his lines is very much like the spacing on a pre-lined piece of paper. We can assume that Gabriel is focused, and that his thoughts are clear and well-organized.

JUMBLED

I let you down. Let me pick you
Let me climb up you to the top
I can see the view from up
there, tangled in your hair.

Lines that intertwine with other lines are poorly spaced. Katrina's words on one line often tangle with those from another line. When writing this sample, Katrina was probably feeling confused. As her thoughts jumbled together, so did her written words. Jumbled lines may also suggest poor organizational skills. At times, graphologists equate jumbled lines with lesser intelligence.

WIDE

ITS BEEN REALLY GREAT LATELY,

WORK HAS BEEN REWARDING —

MY BOSS ACTUALLY SPOKE

WITH ME LATELY AND TOLD

Widely spaced lines are often a sign of good organizational skills, sound judgment and intelligence. Adam's writing indicates that he is probably well-organized and might be an excellent chief executive officer. Buy stock in his company.

Analyzing spacing can be a little tricky. Here's a tip to get you started: With your Spacing Gauge, determine how high and wide the writer's middle zone is. There should be the same approximate space between words. The spacing between letters should look natural to the eye. You probably will not need the Spacing Gauge to determine what type of spacing exists between letters. Decide what categories of spacing Dotti uses. Do you have any new insights into her character?

you know I miss you.
live so far away! I think
Dad. I'm sure you are
New York City sure is a
Cassie and I found a
tiny! Nothing like our huge
I'd say the whole apartn
of your bedroom! we have

CHAPTER NINE

Speed

The speed of a person's writing, which graphologists judge to be either quick or slow, reflects fluidity of thought (or intelligence). Because important words and sentences are written at a different speed than those of less importance, the writer's sincerity can also be evaluated. To a trained eye, the speed with which these key words or sentences have been written is obvious.

Quick writing is typically marked by tall letters, flowing curves and strokes and a rightward slant. When written quickly, the lower-case *i* has a slanted dash for a dot, and the letter *t* has a cross that zooms off the letter to the right.

Slow writing lacks the spontaneity of quick writing and has a more calculated feel. Hence, the slant is either vertical or leftward. When a person writes slowly, the dot above the *i* will be either a distinct dot or a circle, and the *t* crossed carefully and equally on both sides of the letter.

Sorry I didn't get back to you sooner about going to the play but we didn't get back into town

Quick writing is usually not as neat as slow writing, but it is the mark of a mentally balanced and healthy person. We can tell that Tina writes quickly because of the rightward slant, flowing nature and spontaneous appearance of her writing. She dots her *i*'s with slashes and barely touches the letter at all when she crosses her *t*'s. We can assume that Tina is efficient, thinks quickly, and communicates her ideas easily.

*You just a few lines
To let you know I
having a wonderful
Time. Hope you are
having a good Summer
Give my love to the
family*

Slow writing is often the result of a delay between thought and action. Carl's small letters and leftward slant tell us that he writes slowly. Perhaps Carl was unsure of his ideas and how best to communicate them. Carl very much needs to deliberate before speaking and acting. Understandably, the only course Carl ever failed was his freshman debate class.

What do you think about the speed with which Dotti has written? Check her slant, rhythm and how she dots her *i*'s and crosses her *t*'s. Can you detect any significant pauses in her writing? Now try to guess how intelligent and honest Dotti is. We'll compare notes later!

is going well, and I
masters degree in no
teach kindergarten again
nothing is definate yet.
class this year. We have
5 or 6. Mom, the kids
from the kids' at home!
bigger and more worldly
Olivia — seems to know

CHAPTER TEN

Connections

CONNECTIONS

To a graphologist, a connection is the link between letters written in script. (There are no connections between printed letters.) Connections are treasure troves of information, but you have to examine the handwriting samples very closely to identify a subject's connection style. There are many types of connections, but the major categories are: arcades, angles, garlands and threads.

ARCADES

> *I have always wanted to see more of the United States. I've really only been in the*

Arcade connections are arch-like shapes resembling the upper half of a circle. Clarissa's arcade connections reveal that she is superficial. What you see on the surface is not what you really get with Clarissa. Writers who use arcades can sometimes even be crafty, cunning or deceitful. You may already know this, but in case you don't: beware!

going to come your but the

An angle connection is characterized by straight or sharp lines instead of the curves of an arcade. Because angle connections are made when the writer stops and starts writing again, they are not as natural as arcades. The person who uses angle connections is usually ambitious and hard-working, as well as stubborn, persistent and intent on having the last word.

We hope you have a great birthday and enjoy your "24."

The garland connection looks like the bottom half of a circle. A writer who uses garlands is generally flexible, affable, open to compromise and comfortable in social situations.

Thanks very much for my new tie – I love it, really. I even wore it to school before the new tie from Mr. White (But not before Alexendra's Monkey tie). Most of all I love working with you. Thanks for bringing art, smarts, fun, laughter, perspective and

Threaded connections between letters are neither very straight nor very curved. Threads are more difficult to characterize than arcades, angles or garlands. The person who uses threads is easily influenced by others, but is also positive and encouraging—someone who is able to boost your spirits. Threads can also signal an ability to connect without truly committing, and are often associated with diplomacy. Threads, however, can also be associated with duplicity. Threads are considered sneaky—a way for a writer to camouflage his or her intentions.

What does Dotti use to connect her letters—an angle? a thread?
Reminder: Arcade connections are used by writers to cover up and hide.
Angled connections are typical of people who are strict and restrained.
Garlands, with a generally round appearance, are usually associated
with openness and straightforwardness. Threaded connections are
equated with diplomacy as well as with deceitfulness and dishonesty.
I'm sure you're getting a pretty good understanding of Dotti now. Are
Dotti's connections round, angular, thread-like or overhanded and
arcadelike?

bathroom, Kitchen, bedroom,
dining room. And our
any of our friends! Cassie
Most of the decorating.
that kind of stuff. So far
of her artwork, and some

i-Dots
and
t-Bars

Let's say your sister uses big circles to dot her *i*'s and wavy lines to cross her *t*'s while you hardly ever dot an *i* or cross a *t*. Well, maybe it's time to get to the bottom of this manifestation of your basic personality differences. In this chapter you'll learn what graphologists look for when they examine the *i*'s and *t*'s in a handwriting sample.

Remember, before you draw any firm conclusions about your sister (or anyone else), you have to weigh the information gleaned from each handwriting element—the form, zones, spacing and so forth. The need for such thoroughness becomes clear when you consider that the personality traits associated with a circled *i*-dot contradict those associated with a wavy *t*-bar.

When you come across an apparent contradiction in meaning between one handwriting element and another, don't assume that you've misread the handwriting sample. The contradiction merely points to one of the ambiguities inherent in the art and science of handwriting analysis—and it alerts you to tread cautiously as you gather insights about your subject. Don't jump to conclusions, which is something you may be prone to doing if your *t*-bar crosses the air to the right of the stem.

Although the *t*-bar reveals substantial information about a subject's level of drive and ambition, the *i*-dot yields important complementary information. Most people are curious about their goal-orientation, drive and ambition; they will appreciate your thoroughness in considering both the *t*-bar and the *i*-dot when you address this facet of character analysis.

THE *i*-DOT

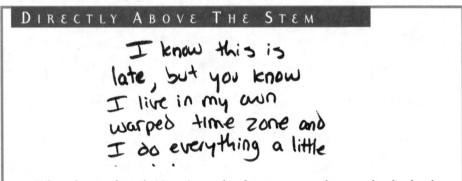

I know this is
late, but you know
I live in my own
warped time zone and
I do everything a little

When dotting her *i*'s, Mary Lou takes her time to make sure the dot lands right above the stem. She considers accuracy to be an important part of her work and self-expression. Her goals are realistic, and she works diligently to achieve them.

ACCENT-LIKE

initially, retirement was set up
young pop. Today there's not
fill the spots.
Today: Social security is shrinking
disappearing, real estate value is
w/ inflation.

Alfred's accent-like dot signifies originality and creativity. He is clever
and imaginative. I was not surprised when he told me that he is a
successful toy inventor.

CURVY OR WAVY

A wavy *i*-dot reveals a spirited and playful nature. The writer loves to have a good time and makes decisions about the future accordingly.

PLACEMENT LEFT OF THE STEM

Like a *t*-bar that crosses to the left of the stem, an *i*-dot above and to the left of the stem reveals that the subject has a cautious nature. This writer is probably fearful of the future and unsure of where he or she might end up.

OPEN-CIRCLE

An *i* that is dotted with a big circle tells us that the writer is childish and immature, probably driven by the need to get attention from others. Decisions are often based on what this writer expects other people will think rather than what is best for him or her personally.

THE t-BAR

How goal-oriented and driven is your subject? You can begin to answer this question by studying the *t*'s in the handwriting sample. Graphologists call the line that crosses the *t* the "*t*-bar." When analyzing the *t*-bar you should consider its length (average, short, long); angle (ascending or descending); shape (curly or looped); and placement (above the stem or to the right or left of the stem).

AVERAGE LENGTH

t The length of this *t*-bar is considered average, which indicates that the writer has set reasonable goals.

SHORT LENGTH

t This short *t*-bar tells us that the writer is not very driven or goal-oriented, but prefers to concentrate on the here and now rather than work for the future.

LONG LENGTH

This long *t*-bar indicates that the writer is driven, determined and willing to work hard.

ASCENDING ANGLE

We can assume, from this ascending *t*-bar, that the writer is looking forward to having an exciting future.

DESCENDING ANGLE

This writer's descending *t*-bar reveals an apprehension about the future.

THE *t*-BAR

CURLY SHAPE

A decorative, curly *t*-bar tells us that this writer is imaginative, inventive, has a whimsical nature, and worries little about what may come.

LOOPED SHAPE

The knot-like shape on this *t*-bar reveals great drive and ambition. The writer is motivated and focused.

PLACEMENT ABOVE THE STEM

A person whose *t*-bar crosses not the actual stem but the air above it is not grounded in reality. Such people make plans for the future that are unrealistic and fantastical.

PLACEMENT LEFT OF THE STEM

People whose *t*-bars cross the air to the left of the stem tend to dwell in the past and have difficulty making decisions about the future. They would rather not contemplate what goals they should be pursuing.

PLACEMENT RIGHT OF THE STEM

A *t*-bar that crosses the air to the right of the stem reveals a person's tendency to be over-excited by potential opportunities and to neglect making sound judgments and careful plans. Such people will act spontaneously—for better or for worse.

Dotti has lots of opportunity to dot her *i*'s and cross her *t*'s when she writes her signature. Compare how she treats these crucial letters in the handwriting sample shown here with the way she handles them in her signature on page 114. What insights are you beginning to gather about Dotti's personality?

Cassie and I found a
tiny! Nothing like our huge
I'd say the whole apart
of your bedroom! we have
bathroom, Kitchen, bedroom,
dining room. And our apar
any of our friends! Cassie
most of the decorating. Yc
that kind of stuff. So far

CHAPTER TWELVE

The Personal Pronoun

THE PERSONAL PRONOUN

How ego-involved is your subject? Look at how he or she writes the personal pronoun *"I"* and you may have your answer.

THE HEIGHT OF THE I

A person's real self-image is revealed in the personal pronoun *"I"*. The taller the *I*, the more highly the subject thinks of himself or herself.

LEFTWARD LEANING

A leftward-slanting *"I"* indicates an inhibited person. If the rest of the writing slants to the right, we assume the writer is struggling to figure out who he or she really is. Most often, this combination of opposing slants identifies a person as conflicted.

A rightward slant indicates a sociable and outgoing personality.

LOOPS IN THE I

WIDE LOOP

Loops in the upper zone of an I indicate autonomy and confidence. The wider the loops, the more egotistical and extroverted the person. This person functions well in social situations but also enjoys being alone.

NARROW LOOP

The narrower the loops in the upper zone, the more reserved and introverted the person.

THE CLASSIC I

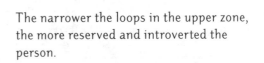

This writer wishes to be understood clearly and easily. A classic I (a straight printed line with two accessory strokes) signifies a reasonable, rational and efficient person who is able to put aside personal feelings and consider the facts. Sounds like he or she would make a good judge, doesn't it?

I bet you've already decided what kind of *I* Dotti uses, but in case you need some help, here's a tip: Look at the height of the *I* and at its direction. Now look for loops and any other unnecessary embellishments. Is it simple and unadorned? Does it appear characteristic of Dotti's other capital letters? I wonder if Dotti would be surprised by your conclusion about the size of her ego?

I am writing to say
you know I miss you.
live so far away! I thi
Dad. I'm sure you a
New York City sure is
Cassie and I found a
tiny! Nothing like our hug
I'd say the whole apar
of your bedroom! We hav

CHAPTER THIRTEEN

Signatures

SIGNATURES

A person's signature can reveal some personality traits that no other handwriting sample can expose. Many handwriting characteristics help indicate who a person really is, but a signature can reveal who a person *wishes* to be.

SIGNATURE THAT MATCHES HANDWRITING

A signature that closely matches the rest of a person's handwriting sample confirms the subject is who he or she claims to be. Stylistically, Marilyn's signature is quite similar to the rest of her handwriting (small to medium size, simple form, quickly written). She is comfortable with who she is and won't go changing herself for anyone—as later attested to by her boyfriend.

shoe salesmen. A lineage of inadequacy
if you ask me. No one cares about
anything I say, or do, or write. But

Bronwin

In general, a very large signature is a sign that the subject wants to be famous—or at least perceived as an important person. Bronwin's signature, which is much larger than the rest of her writing, suggests that she has high hopes and big dreams. It's clear from her personal pronoun *I* (with wide loops) that she craves attention.

If i had two oranges,
i would eat two oranges?

Seth's signature, which is much smaller than the rest of his handwriting, tells us he doesn't want to call attention to himself. It's possible that Seth may be quite smitten with himself, but he doesn't want to be viewed as arrogant or conceited. It's also possible that Seth is an extremely modest guy, believing himself unworthy of a look-at-me signature. This can be confirmed by examining Seth's personal pronoun *I*.

An illegible signature is often the sign of an egotist—someone who expects other people to know who he is or to take the time to figure it out. It also can reveal a person who is affected and pretentious. Beckett's scrawl tells us that he's impatient—that he believes his time is more valuable than anyone else's. If Beckett's form were "counterfeit," we would know he was a show off, but since his form is simplistic, we can assume he may just be pressed for time.

Annie Birch

Annie's signature tells us that she is conventional—she follows the rules and does as she's told. She's using a formulaic style to identify herself and isn't concerned about being perceived as less than creative.

I wish I wasn't so busy here lately. As soon as I catch up on some of my work maybe we can get together for a cup of coffee.

Connie

When a signature slants differently from a person's handwriting, it's an indication of some inner conflict. Note that though Connie's signature slants to the right, the rest of her handwriting slants to the left. Connie is sending a subconscious signal that she is outgoing and extroverted, when, in reality, she is introverted.

Wesley's signature is full of flourishes and decorations—a clear sign of a very big ego and a deep desire to be noticed.

A box or circle around a signature functions as a shield—guarding and protecting a person against intrusion. Here we see that Carmine is sensitive and cautious—fearful of losing his privacy.

How does Dotti sign off on her communications? Try comparing her signature to Bronwin's, to Marilyn's, and so forth. Here's a tip for analyzing this very personal signal about a person's character: Analyzing a signature separate from its surrounding text can be less accurate than when you have other copy for comparison. Examine Dotti's signature relative to the rest of her letters. Are there any inconsistencies between her other writing and her signature? Finding any differences will help you assess Dotti's public persona.

well, although from from you last month. It Please send my love to Chip. Tell them all tha much. I hope to hear

love,

Dotti

CHAPTER FOURTEEN

Sample Analysis

Dear Mom,

I am writing to say "hello," and let you know I miss you. It's too bad we live so far away! I think of you often, and Dad. I'm sure you are doing well. ~~It's~~ New York City sure is a fun city to live in! Cassie and I found a place to live - it's tiny! Nothing like our huge farm in Nebraska. I'd say the whole apartment is the size of your bedroom! We have 5 rooms: a bathroom, kitchen, bedroom, living room, and dining room. And our apartment is larger than any of our friends'! Cassie has taken care of most of the decorating. You know how she loves that kind of stuff. So far she's put up a lot of her artwork, and some of my black and white photographs. We were able to get some really cheap furniture from a thrift shop nearby. We've made a lot of friends already, mostly from our jobs. Her art is really starting to sell! She is having an exhibit in Soho next month. Maybe you and Dad could come! We have a fold out couch in the living room. How are Brian and Little Chip? It's been so long since I've heard from them. Tell them to call me already - they are my brothers, after all. So, things with John are great! We're planning a huge vacation

HANDWRITING ANALYSIS

to Italy. He loves it there, and had promised to be my personal tour guide. We plan to go sometime this summer, since I have 3 months off from teaching. John has to work all summer, but we plan to rent a house somewhere for the weekends. School is going well, and I should have my masters degree in no time. I hope to teach Kindergarten again next year, although nothing is definate yet. I have a great class this year. We have 23 kids, all ages 5 or 6. Mom, the kids here are so different from the kids at home! They seem so much bigger and more worldly. My favorite girl - Olivia - seems to know more than the fifth graders I taught at home. And Alex is the same way. He's only 6, but can read fluently and writes stories. I've never seen anything like it! Well, that's about it. I hope you are doing well, although from the letter I recieved from you last month, it sounds like you are. Please send my love to Dad, Brian, and Little Chip. Tell them all that I love them very much. I hope to hear from you soon.

Love,

Dotti

I don't know Dotti personally, and before analyzing her sample of handwriting I was told only that she is a young woman who recently moved to New York City.

As I suggested earlier, it is best not to read the content of the handwriting sample you plan to analyze before examining its physical appearance. (I must admit that it was very nice to discover, after finishing my analysis, that the content matches quite closely what I deduced.)

First, I looked at the form of Dotti's handwriting. Because it is clear and legible, yet slightly decorative, I have categorized her as artistic. As you might remember, an artistic form is often associated with people who are creative and of high intelligence.

Next, I examined Dotti's use of zones. For the most part, Dotti's middle zone is much larger than her upper or lower zones. A large middle zone signifies that a person is passionate and concerned more about the present than either the past or the future.

Dotti has a straight baseline throughout most of the letter. Only at the very end do a couple of the lines descend. I believe that Dotti is neither overly optimistic nor pessimistic. However, at the tail end of her letter, she grew somewhat frustrated, dissuaded or exhausted.

Dotti's writing pressure is heavy, with her downstrokes heavier than her upstrokes. Because pressure reveals a person's stamina and drive, I presume that Dotti is intense and forceful, at times even outspoken.

Dottie does not always connect her letters. Sometimes she has written in script, and at other times she has written in print. When she does connect her letters, she uses garlands, signifying a person who performs well in social situations. The fact that she does not always connect her letters, however, is also significant. Dottie may not wish to relate to others all the time. Or, perhaps she does not always feel entirely comfortable when relating to others.

A vertical slant, like Dotti's, tells us that a person is independent. Dotti probably does not share her emotions with many people. A vertical slant is also associated with those who live in the present. This helps me confirm my earlier hypothesis that Dotti is oriented in the here and now.

Letter size reveals a writer's ability to concentrate. The majority of graphologists agree that medium-sized letters with garland connects are ideal. Dotti writes with both, telling us that she has little difficulty concentrating and is quite capable of adjusting to change.

While Dotti's spacing between letters is normal, her spacing between lines is a little on the narrow side. Because she dots her *i*'s with open circles, her writing has a jumbled appearance. Jumbled lines signify jumbled thoughts.

I am also going to assume that Dotti's handwriting is neither quick nor slow. It has a natural and fluid appearance, which would suggest a quick pace. However, she stops and takes time to dot her *i*'s with circles, which would slow her writing down considerably. This probably means that appearance is of more importance to Dotti than efficiency.

In chapter 11 (*i-Dots* and *t-Bars*), I suggested you examine the way that Dotti crosses her *t*'s. The descending *t*-bar warns us that Dotti is apprehensive about her future. This is another reason why she may dwell in the present.

Dotti's personal pronoun *I*'s are on the small side, sometimes smaller than other letters without any upper zone at all. The height of the personal pronoun will often reveal how a person feels about himself or herself. We can assume that Dotti is not overly confident.

But she sure wants others to think well of her! Dotti's signature is much larger than the rest of her text—meaning she wants to be noticed and considered important. Her signature is also more inclined than the rest of her writing, signaling that she wants others to believe she is more extroverted than she really is.

Now take a look at the content. These hypotheses seem pretty accurate, don't they?

A young woman who recently arrived in New York City from a farm in Nebraska might very well feel all the ways Dotti seems to. Of course, the present is all she has time to think about. Such a dramatic relocation could be very taxing on anyone.

She is clearly creative, as we guessed earlier. (See the reference to her photography.)

Dotti is neither pessimistic nor optimistic, but the descending baseline at the very end gives us a glimpse into what might be Dotti's apprehension. Will she really make it in the big city after all?

The vertical slant makes sense, too. Dottie must be independent if she uprooted herself and chose to live in a busy and unfamiliar environment.

I also guessed earlier that Dotti is capable of adjusting well to change. She sure doesn't seem overly homesick in her letter to her mom and dad.

And of course she wants to be noticed and be considered important. New York City can certainly make people feel insignificant.

I wish Dotti luck, though I get the feeling she'll be just fine. (I'd be fine, too, if I had a boyfriend about to whisk me off to Europe!)

CHAPTER FIFTEEN

Celebrity Handwriting

CELEBRITY HANDWRITING

The people whose handwriting samples appear in this chapter have well-known public personae. In some cases the handwriting looks the way we might expect it to look; in other cases, it seems an unlikely match between the writer and the handwriting.

Clearly, it would be impossible to attempt a definitive character analysis based on the brief samples shown here. Still, it's fun to peer into the flourishes, slants, and baselines of well-known people . . . and to wonder what might lurk between the lines.

Included in the following pages are several categories of handwriting samples: text only, text plus signature and signature only. The more skills you learned in chapters 2 through 13, the more insights you'll be able to derive from these samples.

NAME THE AUTHOR

To emphasize how misleading our expectations about handwriting can be, we've included five samples of handwriting minus the signatures. The samples were written by the following well-known people: Sigmund Freud, Nicole Brown Simpson, Jacqueline Kennedy Onassis, Elvis Presley, and Mother Theresa.

Each sample is identified by a number. Judging by what you know of the celebrities' public personae, try matching the samples to the authors—and try not to use the content of the message as a clue to the writer's identity. The correct answers are given at the end of this chapter.

SUBJECT NO. 1

People whose writing rises upward and to the right of the baseline, as shown here, are generally energetic. It is safe to say that Subject No. 1 was capable of accomplishing several different things at once. The spacing of the letters and the zones are also significant in this sample.

help me turn negatives into p
help me get rid of my anger
learned to "let things go"
powerful, helpful thing she
she learned that all thing
& bother me, are just a m
going on in me. I always
what was going on with us

This subject has a very large middle zone, which is common of people who are comfortable inhabiting present time; they do not dwell in the past or worry about the future. They may have a secure and passionate nature, which when exaggerated can tend toward egotism and perhaps immaturity.

HANDWRITING ANALYSIS

I Love it. Sir. I can and will be of any service that I can to help the country out. I have no concern or motives other than helping the country out. So Insist not to be given a title or an appointment. I can and will do more good if I were

Consider the connecting strokes in this sample. They are straight, sharp lines rather than curved. The writer was most likely hard-working and persistent—qualities that, when taken to extreme, can become self-defeating stubbornness.

preparing for their profession. The first 10 - will be professed on the 12ᵗʰ April. They will make their Vows for one year — I will make my final Vows on the same day

The baseline in this sample is erratic; it goes every which way. The writer may well have been moody and very emotional. Such sensitivity often leads to empathy, but when exaggerated in a negative direction can turn into an unstable quality that puts the person at the mercy of external forces.

Dear Kamande Gatura –

I would like to tell you how much – so far away in Kenya, means to us in the writings of your "parent", Baroness Karen

I have read all her books – and al

Now Peter Beard has shown me yo It makes me wish that I knew your coun' to my children. Each evening they ask me

Writing that is small in size is a sign of someone who values privacy, never intentionally seeking the spotlight. The personal pronoun I's have a leftward slant, further reinforcing this person's inhibited nature.

SIGNATURE VS. TEXT

In this section you'll find samples of text plus signatures. Notice how often the writing in the signature differs from that in the text—a sure sign that the writer wishes to be a certain personality type but is, in fact, quite another.

TIMOTHY MCVEIGH

New York State Penal Law. Sure enough, 270 prohibits possession of any noxious substance, included in section 265 is a ban on the of "stun guns". Now I am a male, and fully capable of physically defending myself; how about a female?

McVeigh's leftward slant tells us that he represses his emotions. It also tells us that he has negative, fearful and resistant feelings. Leftward slants often indicate an obsession with the past. Timothy McVeigh's writing is also characterized by wide spacing between his words. This indicates a need for personal space and distance from others. His signature is illegible, which is often the sign of an egotist or a person who is affected and pretentious.

Bill Clinton

*Thanks so much for your
letter. & welcome your ideas,
They will be carefully
considered. I'm grateful
you took the time to write.*

Bill

President Clinton's heavy downstrokes reveal his incredible stamina, energy and work ethic. Notice the short *l*'s contrast with the emphasis on the descender of the *y*'s. His writing emphasizes the lower zone, which often signifies a strong concern with the physical self.

I do hope you will write to me and tell me all about yourself. I know I haven't kept up my correspondence in past very well, but I intend to do so in the future so please do write and let me know how you are.

You will be seeing more of me soon in — "Lets' Make Love"

please help me — if Dr. Kris assured you I am allright — you can assure her I am not. I do not belong here!

happy Christmas - Mr. Sinatra, you know my friend "Frank — also asks

We have a few different samples of Ms. Monroe's handwriting. You can see how it developed and changed over the years. Her slant moved from leftward to rightward. Her personal pronouns changed from a single-lined *I* (an honest and simple representation of self) to a more ornate one. Graphologists equate the *I* shown here with rebelliousness.

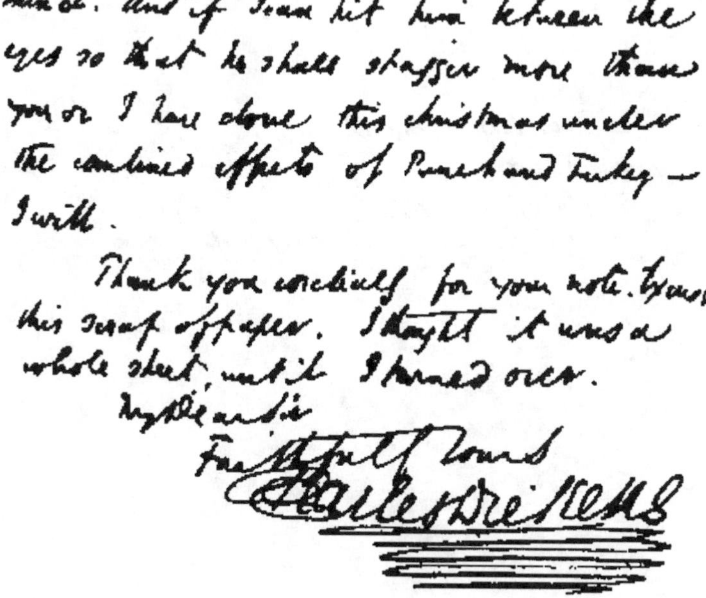

mind. And if I can hit him between the eyes so that he shall stagger more than you or I have done this Christmas under the combined effects of Punch and Turkey — I will.

Thank you cordially for your note. Excuse this scrap of paper. I thought it was a whole sheet, until I turned over.

My Dear Sir

Faithfully Yours

Charles Dickens

Dickens's heavily underscored signature tells us that he was self-assertive and resolute. It had to be his way or no way. Is this personality trait also found in the text of his writing?

des liens plus etroit et plus
doux ceux de l'amitié et de
la reconnoifsance
le 1.er fevrier 1792   Marie Antoinette

While Marie Antoinette's writing is in cursive, her signature is in printed letters. This change of style indicates her wish to keep her public self separate from her true self. The lack of any connecting strokes in her signature was her way of keeping her distance from others.

Mozart's signature is underscored with one simple line. This tells us that he was secure and confident, yet not as egotistical as he might have been had his signature been underscored more times than once. The text and signature appear similar in many respects: slant, spacing, size and zone. We can't judge the pressure or form, and speed is difficult to gauge with such a short sample of handwriting. But it appears that who he wished to be and who he was are well-aligned.

Gandhi's ascending signature indicates that he was positive, active and content with his public persona. An ascending signature is common among people who view their careers as blossoming. It's hard to say if this analysis would be confirmed in a longer sample of text.

unhappy in my genius, having rose above
vulgar superstition of the human race, and
fallen, below the understanding of the learn
and wife. However I submit the Book t
ur Lordships candor. and am with the
eatest respect and esteem,

My Lord, your
Lordships most devoted, Obedient and
Humble Servant. Ethan Allen

Ethan Allen's lines overlap one another. Tangled lines like his often equate with jumbled thoughts and an inability to concentrate (or, with a scarce supply of paper). However, the spacing and slant are consistent throughout the sample. The general appearance is similar to counterfeit form, as seen in the loops and other flourishes. A definitive analysis would require careful weighing of all elements of the handwriting.

*order them therefore freely: you know they
it to their delicacy. I am looking forward
then I can embrace you in all my affection
occupies much of my thoughts as the
affectionately to mrs Randolph, and he*

Th: Jefferson

Jefferson's personal pronoun *I* is a line with an upper loop and no base. Such an *I* indicates a strong identification with a father figure and an early life that had a strong influence on him in later years. This type of personal pronoun *I* is also common among those who are idealistic.

Sorry Dear that you are ill
Hurry get well soon and do that
Real soon

Lady Day

Billie Holiday

Billie Holiday's signature slashes itself. This handwriting trait is common among people who are trying to destroy or harm themselves in some way.

I have read the paper by Mr Francis Upton and it is the first correct and authoritative account of my invention of the Electric Light

Yours Truly

Thomas A Edison.

Menlo Park N.J.

Thomas Edison's signature has an overscore. Overscores are much less common than underscores. They are associated with egotism, but are often also considered a compensatory effort stemming from self-doubt and insecurity.

DOLLY PARTON

Dolly Parton's signature has a circle around it. This circling-in of her name indicates a possible fear of intrusion. The circle acts like a shield around someone who worries about her privacy.

BEATRIX POTTER

Beatrix Potter's simple and unadorned signature tells us that she was not preoccupied with her public persona.

Queen Elizabeth I signed her name in a very fancy and ornate fashion. The many unnecessary underscores and overscores signify an affected nature and egotistical view.

IVANA TRUMP

Ivana Trump connects her letters with arcades. Arcade connections reveal a person's need to dominate and control. They also tell us that the subject is an independent thinker who is not prone to change her mind for the sake of others.

Muhammad Ali's signature is extreme in its upper and lower zones. The large upper zone tells us that he lives in a fantasy world. His long reach into the lower zone reveals a life concerned with physical and superficial needs. (Large lower zones are typical of many athletes.)

MARTIN LUTHER KING, JR.

Dr. King wrote with a heavy pressure. This heavy pressure confirms what we already know of him: that he was intense, determined and dynamic.

CLAUDE MONET

Claude Monet's handwriting is characterized by wide spacing between letters. Such spacing indicates a person who wishes to maintain his or her distance from others—a reclusive trait.

STING

We can compare two signatures of the musician Sting (originally G.M. Summer). His earlier one had a small middle zone, indicating dissatisfaction with his everyday life. The later signature is more zonally balanced. The upper zone is no longer so high, revealing that his feet have landed on the ground and his fantasy world has become more of a reality.

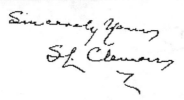

Clemens's wavy underscore is lively and spirited. (Clemens is perhaps better known as Mark Twain.) A wavy underscore is considered a sign of self-importance.

Napoleon's signature underwent many changes throughout his lifetime, from legible to illegible. It also acquired an underscore that slashed through itself. Again, this crossing out of one's own signature is a very self-destructive sign.

P S E U D O N Y M S

When an author uses a pseudonym, there is a conscious decision to portray a masked identity. Arriving at a character analysis in such cases is probably unwise. Here we see that Charles Dodgson signed his name and his pseudonym (Lewis Carroll) with some similar touches. For example, the *C* in both names has an enclosing quality. Such circling often indicates a fear of intrusion. However, the *L* and *C* are, in both names, much larger than the other letters. This exaggeration in size of the capital letters in a signature reveals a person's wish to be perceived by others as great. It is also a sign of high self-esteem.

CHARLES DODGSON/LEWIS CARROLL

ANSWERS TO "NAME THE AUTHOR"
1. Freud 2. Simpson 3. Presley 4. Mother Theresa 5. Onassis

CHAPTER SIXTEEN

Fun Facts
and Tips

- Strangely formed loops in the lower zone can indicate guilt about a person's sex drive.
- A *t*-bar that hovers above the letter is an indicator that the writer lives in a fantasy world.
- Some graphologists believe that a signature that crosses like an *x* underneath is a sign of suicidal tendencies.
- When a doodler draws a face that looks to the left, it is a sign that he or she is thinking about the past.
- Edgar Allen Poe was a graphologist.
- Graphology appears in the text of Robert Louis Stevenson's *The Strange Case of Dr. Jekyll and Mr. Hyde.*
- The use of drugs and alcohol can completely alter the appearance of a person's handwriting.
- As people age, their connecting strokes between letters deteriorate.
- Too many underscores and too much punctuation can signify a hypochondriac.
- When a writer's pressure is extremely heavy or extremely light, it can sometimes indicate mental illness.
- *T*-bars that cross up to the right can reveal that the subject is a social climber.
- Beware of excessive punctuation. It may mean that the writer was faking enthusiasm when he or she sent you that birthday card.

TIPS

- To keep yourself as unbiased as possible, analyze the appearance of the writing first. If you consider the content first, you may form preconceptions about your subject.
- It's best to get handwriting samples written on unlined paper. Writing on unlined paper, the author must choose his or her own spacing—and spacing can reveal a lot about a person's relations with others.
- If possible, encourage your subject to use a ballpoint pen or sharpened pencil. It is difficult to examine the pressure and form of writing done with felt-tipped pens and markers.
- If possible, make note of the subject's age, sex and occupation. This information cannot be determined from handwriting but may be useful when making your final evaluation of your subject's personality and character traits.
- Handwriting analyses are most accurate when you work with at least a half a page of text followed by your subject's signature. Just comparing the writing and the signature can be quite revealing.
- Make copies of the samples you wish to analyze. You may make mistakes and you should not clutter the original with commentary that may prove distracting.

USING YOUR TOOLS

Throughout this book, you probably have been experimenting with your three special "tools of the trade." Following are some tips for exactly how and when to use them.

THE EMOTION QUOTIENT GAUGE

Yes, your Emotion Quotient Gauge (EQ Gauge) does resemble that protractor you used back in high school. But I'm sure you'll have much more fun measuring personality traits than you had measuring angles.

Your EQ Gauge is actually quite simple to use. Here's all you do:

1. Place the EQ Gauge over the portion of handwriting you wish to assess.

2. Line up the baseline of the EQ Gauge so that it overlays the baseline of a line of handwriting.

3. Examine the angle of the letters of handwriting according to the EQ Gauge. Do they fall in the "overly inclined" section or do they fit neatly into the "vertical section"? Make your decision.

4. Now you can determine how expressive your subject is. Just read the section on slants (chapter 6) and you'll be an expert at assessing a person's expressiveness in no time.

SPACING GAUGE

Your Spacing Gauge will prove handy when you examine the three zones of writing. As you learned in chapter 3, all letters are divided into three zones: the upper, middle and lower zones. When studying this chapter, you can use your Spacing Gauge to make more exact measurements. Here's how:

1. First, you should measure the upper zone. Let's say that the upper zone measures 1/2" (12-16 millimeters).
2. Next you should measure the lower zone. In order to determine zonal balance, the lower zone should also measure 1/2" (12-16 millimeters).
Technically, a zonally balanced writer will have upper and lower zones of equal measurement.
3. Now you must measure the middle zone. The middle zone should have a 1/4" (6-8 millimeters) measurement. To be considered zonally balanced, the middle zone should measure one half that of the upper zone and one half that of the lower zone.

The ideal ratio of zone heights is:

Upper zone: 1
Lower zone: 1
Middle zone: 1/2

If the middle zone is much larger or smaller than one half the upper or lower zone, your subject lacks zonal balance. Refer to the chapter on zones and find out exactly what that means.

MAGNIFYING GLASS

Your magnifying glass will come in handy when analyzing connections, as well as when examining very small writing and letters that run together.

BIBLIOGRAPHY

Amend, Karen and Mary S. Ruiz. *Handwriting Analysis: The Complete Basic Book.* North Hollywood, California: Newcastle Publishing Co., Inc., 1980.

Branston, Barry. *Graphology Explained: A Workbook.* York Beach, Maine: Samuel Weiser, Inc., 1991.

Gardner, Ruth. *Instant Handwriting Analysis: A Key to Personal Success.* St. Paul, Minnesota: Llewellyn Publications, 1997.

Hayes, Reed. *Between the Lines: Understanding Yourself and Others Through Handwriting Analysis.* Rochester, Vermont: Destiny Books, 1993.

Hollander, P. Scott. *Handwriting Analysis.* St. Paul, Minnesota: Llewellyn Publications, 1998.

Mahony, Ann. *Handwriting and Personality: How Graphology Reveals What Makes People Tick.* New York: Ivy Books, 1989.

McNichol, Andrea with Jeffrey A. Nelson. *Handwriting Analysis: Putting It to Work for You.* Chicago, Illinois: Contemporary Books, 1991.

Olyanova, Nadya. *The Psychology of Handwriting: Secrets of Handwriting Analysis.* North Hollywood, California: Sterling Publishing Co., Inc., 1960.

Peters, Cash. *Instant Insight: Secrets of Life, Love, and Your Destiny Revealed in Your Handwriting.* New York: Warner Books, 1998.

Santoy, Claude. *The ABCs of Handwriting Analysis.* New York: Marlowe Company, 1994.